朱利安 飢餓的白蜘蛛

由大衛·達塞利·桑塔納撰寫

視覺藝術插畫家：

- **Artisto Work**（首席 第一的 和 首席藝術創作者）

- **大衛·D·桑塔納**（第二 號校長和 藝術品 的最終編輯）

- **馬科斯·伊格納西奧·桑塔納**（校長 第三 和主要著色創建者）

藝術時代背景與人物形象化...深愛的...

- **瑪麗亞路易莎 阿維萊斯 菲耶羅 Larrinaga 麥德林**

所有藝術品和故事 (C) 大衛·Darseli·桑塔納, Darseli 圖書出版。版權所有。

大衛·Darseli·桑塔納 和 Darseli 圖書出版 的律師：

P.C. Dinah Perez 律師事務所
　　　世紀公園東 1801 號套房 2400
　　　加利福尼亞州洛杉磯 90067

未經版權所有者的法律明確書面公證許可,不得複製、存儲在檢索系統中或以任何形式或通過任何方式(電子、機械、影印、錄音、互聯網或其他方式)傳輸本書的任何部分。

朱利安 飢餓的白蜘蛛 (中文) ISBN: 978-0-9896914-6-8
　　出版商識別序列號：2022DBPJULIAN1968MARCH7CHINESE-PF

致謝:特別感謝"wework"及其主要創始人 Miguel McKelvey、Adam Neumann 和 Adam 的妻子 Rebekah Victoria Neumann Paltrow。他們的共同願景創造了一個有趣且有益的工作環境……人們也受到周圍所有為實現個人目標而努力的人的啟發!儘管故事和所有藝術品都是在我的家中創作的,但我在 2022 年對 Julian The White Hungry Spider 的最後一次編輯發生在"wework"。為它的創始人和當時和現在所有參與其中的人鼓掌,他們在創造如此偉大的"工作"環境中突破極限!去""我們工作""！！！而且,最重要的是,感謝天父永遠愛我們。

　　這本書的副本是出版商副本。此書名的所有圖書副本均為出版商(Darseli Book Publishing)的專有財產。只能通過許可訪問本書和任何 DBP 書籍及其各自的"媒體"副本。要獲得此標題的訪問權限,您必須同意以下 3 頁(以及發布商官方網站)中的最終用戶許可協議(也稱為 EULA)。接受本 EULA 併購買許可證後,您可以獲得對本 DBP 知識產權的訪問權。

　　請仔細閱讀以下 3 個 EULA 頁面>>> 以了解如何訪問此知識產權的發布者副本(可在發布者網站 Darseli.Com 上找到可更新的 EULA 或通過請求發送至：MiCostaBella@Gmail.Com。

Darseli Book Publishing's
最終用戶許可協議 (EULA)

Darseli 圖書出版（也稱為 DBP 或 Publisher）最終用戶許可協議 (EULA)。 EULA 也稱為許可協議或書籍許可協議或協議。請在購買 DBP 許可以訪問此 DBP 產品和出版商擁有的紙張（或其他）"中"之前仔細閱讀此和以下英語 EULA（DBP 許可協議）。 DBP 圖書許可協議也稱為協議、許可、有限許可、最終用戶許可協議、EULA 等。在完全接受本協議並隨後購買 DBP 許可後，DBP 授予您有限的、個人的、非排他性的、不可轉讓的和可撤銷的許可（無再許可權），以訪問此指定的 DBP 產品（知識產權）及其相應的出版商擁有的與購買的特定許可證相關的紙（或其他）"媒體"。如果您不完全接受本許可協議 (EULA)，則不能授予您訪問任何 DBP 產品和此指定 DBP 產品及其相應的出版商擁有的紙（或其他）"媒介"的許可（或維持許可）由出版商。因此，您將無法訪問指定的 DBP 產品或其相應的"媒介"。本文（或其他）"中"（出版商擁有的副本）始終是出版商的專有財產，不得出售。僅授予您訪問本 EULA 的出版商擁有的"中等"副本的許可。本許可應僅被解釋為許可協議，此處未明確授予的任何權利均由發布者保留並歸發布者所有。如果您需要本 EULA 的禮貌翻譯，請將您的請求發送至：MiCostaBella@Gmail.Com。請繼續閱讀完整的英文 EULA，以便繼續獲得或保持有效的許可證以訪問此產品和任何 DBP 產品以及相應的媒體：

Darseli Book Publishing's End User License Agreement (EULA)
Darseli Book Publishing (also known as DBP or Publisher) End User License Agreement (EULA). EULA also referred to as license agreement or book license agreement or agreement. PLEASE READ THIS EULA (DBP BOOK LICENSE AGREEMENT) CAREFULLY BEFORE PURCHASING a DBP LICENSE. DBP Book License Agreement also known as AGREEMENT, LICENSE, LIMITED LICENSE, End User License Agreement, EULA, and similar. Upon Full Acceptance of this agreement, and the purchase of a DBP license thereafter, DBP grants you a limited, personal, non-exclusive, non-transferable and revocable license (without the right to sublicense) to access a specified DBP product (intellectual property) and its respective and corresponding Publisher owned "Medium" related to the specific license purchased. Without your FULL ACCEPTANCE of this license agreement (EULA), an issuance of a license to access the DBP product specified and its corresponding Publisher owned "Medium" cannot be granted to you by the Publisher. Hence, you will not have access to the specified DBP product or its corresponding "Medium". This License shall be construed as a license agreement only, and any rights not expressly granted herein are reserved by and to the Publisher.
Specific DBP product in this License Agreement (but EULA pertains to any DBP product):

朱利安 飢餓的白蜘蛛 [Julian The Hungry Spider]
(hereinbefore and and hereinhere and hereafter referred to as book, the book, intellectual property, licensed intellectual property, DBP product, or similar references.):
朱利安 飢餓的白蜘蛛 (中文) ISBN: 978-0-9896914-6-8
出版商識別序列號：2022DBPJULIAN1968MARCH7CHINESE-PF

EULA SECTION ILA (Sec. 1 of 9): Introduction Agreement To License:
ILA 1: Darseli Book Publishing is hereinbefore and hereinhere and hereafter referred to as, but not limited to: Publisher, us, our, DBP, Darseli Book Publishing, Grantor, intellectual property owner, author, Licensor, or similar references.
ILA 2: You the potential license buyer or purchaser or non-purchaser of the License to access the DBP product or book and its corresponding Publisher Owned "Medium" in this license agreement is referred to but not limited to: "I", the licensee, purchaser, you, your, and similar references.
ILA 3: By purchasing a license to access the DBP product or book (licensed intellectual property) listed above (or any DBP product) and its corresponding "Medium" you FULLY agree to the terms and conditions of this license agreement INCLUDING, WITHOUT LIMITATION, THE PROVISIONS ON LICENSE RESTRICTION, which began above and continues below. By your full agreement of this EULA you may purchase a license to come into access of a specified DBP product or book and its corresponding "Medium" (Medium owned perpetually by the Publisher).
ILA 4: Hereinbefore and hereinhere and hereinafter, the DBP product's or book's "Medium" refers to the medium used to house or place the intellectual property on such as but not limited to: paper medium, electronic medium, and so forth. If you came upon the book or its corresponding "Medium" without the purchase of a license, you are not authorize to use this intellectual property and its corresponding "Medium" which is property of the Publisher at all times and places. That is, the "Medium" (as well as the book or DBP product) remains at all times and places exclusive property of the Publisher. Accordingly, you Understand and Agree that this book and its "Medium" is NOT for SALE. The License purchased only grants you access to the book and its corresponding "Medium" in accordance to this EULA which describes among other items the restrictions of use of the book or DBP product and its corresponding "Medium".
ILA 5: You understand and agree that If you purchased the license to access a DBP product or book (intellectual property) and its corresponding "medium" format (paper or otherwise) and do not agree with the terms of this license agreement (EULA) after rereading them, return the intellectual property and its "Medium" within 34 days for a full LICENSE FEE refund (subject to DBP's Return Policy Found at Darseli.Com) TO THE PLACE WHERE YOU OBTAINED IT (be it either from the Publisher OR ITS AUTHORIZED AGENT (current DBP Authorized Agents listed at Darseli.Com, or by emailing us and requesting the current DBP Authorized Agents list to: MiCostaBella@Gmail.Com).

The DBP product or book and its corresponding "medium" MUST BE RETURNED at the time of refund request, and our authorization to do so, AND BEFORE REFUND in order to receive a LICENSE FEE refund. Shipping expense for the return of the licensed book and its "Medium" is at your expense if shipping is necessary. After the 34 days, NO REFUND of license fee is granted even if the Publisher terminates your license to use the book (DBP product) and its corresponding "Medium" for any reason including violation of this license agreement or suspected violation of this license agreement or for any other reason or for no reason.

Additionally, you understand and agree to re-read and FULLY agree to the full elaborate complete, and up to date EULA found at www.Darseli.Com, or by requesting the full current DBP EULA at MiCostaBella@Gmail.Com within 20 days of license purchase.
ILA 6-Sub 1: Full refund applies only to "PAPER" medium format or similar Tangible "Medium" format of the book (DBP product). Intangible format of the book (such as electronic "Medium" format of the book and similar) are NOT entitled for refund even if your license to use the book is terminated by Publisher for violation or suspected violation of the book license agreement or for any reason or no reason, or by your disagreement with the full book license agreement (EULA).
ILA 6-Sub 2: Accordingly, for such intangible "Medium" format such as "electronic" format (and tangible "Medium" formats such as "paper"), the Publisher STRONGLY advises the potential purchaser of a DBP license to CAREFULLY read the license agreement in full, understand it completely, and FULLY agree with it completely BEFORE purchasing a DBP license to access any DBP product and its corresponding "medium".
ILA 7: This is an agreement made between you, the entity in possession or to be in possession of our intellectual property and its corresponding "Medium" via the purchase of a license or the license purchaser or potential purchaser of the license or entity in possession of our book and its "Medium" (irrespective of being authorized or not) AND the Publisher of the DBP product or book.
ILA 8: An entity may not purchase a license to access the DBP product or book and its corresponding medium if the entity is not considered a legal adult in their country of origin where they are a citizen.

Minors living under the same physical residence of the legal adult purchaser of a DBP license, may access the DBP product or book and its corresponding "Medium" for personal use only and as outlined in this license agreement. The minor must be supervised at all times by the DBP license purchaser when using any DBP product including books and their corresponding medium. And the DBP license purchaser is responsible for the acts of the minor that go against the interest of the Publisher and its intellectual property and corresponding mediums and the EULA. You fully agree that Any violation by the minor against this EULA makes the purchaser of a DBP license and its corresponding medium fully liable. Purchaser is the DBP license buyer granted access to the DBP product or the book and its corresponding "Medium". The purchaser is also the entity that has agreed to this EULA and proceeded to purchase a DBP license to access the Publisher's intellectual property and its corresponding medium.

ILA 9: This license agreement to access the DBP product and its corresponding "Medium" is NOT a contract for sale and or rent of a DBP product or book or its corresponding "Medium": RATHER, it is a license to access and use a DBP product or book and its corresponding "Medium" subject to the terms and conditions of this Agreement (EULA). The DBP product or book and its corresponding "Medium" is licensed NOT SOLD.

ILA 10: You fully agree that The DBP product or book and its corresponding "Medium" (physical or non-physical) (in paper, plastic, electronic format, or otherwise) is always property of the Publisher and cannot be transferred by the licensee or third party or any other entity at anytime or place. You also understand and fully agree that the DBP product or book and its corresponding "Medium" provided is Not for you to give-away, sale, rent, license, sublicense, transfer, delegate, or otherwise at any time and at any location by you or a third party or any entity be it at a physical place, the Internet or otherwise (said items always remain exclusive property of the Publisher). You also fully agree that You are only granted a license to access and use the intellectual property and its "Medium" for personal use only and as to the terms of this agreement.

ILA 11: Please read the terms and conditions above and below carefully.

DBP and you agree on the above and the below sections and everything in it. If you do not FULLY agree with this EULA, you may not purchase a license to use any DBP product or book and its corresponding "Medium" or maintain the book and its corresponding "medium" in your possession. Furthermore, No entity may have in its/his/her possession any DBP product or book and its corresponding "Medium" without having a purchased Publisher granted license to access them unless otherwise stated in this EULA.

EULA SECTION NTI (Sec. 2 of 9):: Non-Transferable Disclosure (NTD)

NTD 1: You may have an additional notarized written agreement directly with Publisher (for example: a volume license agreement) that only supplements this agreement. You agree that In no way does any other written agreement with the Publisher contradict the core of this license agreement including the understanding that the publisher maintains at all times and places exclusive ownership of the DBP product or book and its corresponding "Medium", and you agree that the license restrictions and all other restrictions in this license agreement (EULA) are preserved in any other additional written agreement that may be made by the Publisher and you or other entity (including an entity that is granted status by the Publisher as an Authorized Agent of the Publisher).

NTD 2: Limited Rights. Upon payment of the nonrefundable DBP license fee (refundable only within 34 days as stated earlier for paper "medium" format only), you agree that DBP grants you a limited, non-exclusive, revocable, nontransferable license to use a particular respective DBP product or book (intellectual property) and its corresponding "Medium". You agree that any authorized agent granted by the Publisher must follow the core outline of this EULA as well at all times.

EULA SECTION NDPA (Sec. 3 of 9): No Distribution Permitted Agreement (NDPA):

NDPA 1: This Agreement describes the terms governing your use of the DBP product or book (intellectual property), intellectual property content, and the corresponding "Medium" in any format.

NDPA 2A: You and any other entity further and additionally FULLY agree, understand, and accept that the United States (U.S.) Copyright Law SECTION § 109, and also in particular its (§ 109) subsection (a) and (c) (or any other nation similar section) do not apply to this agreement or any DBP product; and you and any other entity who may be in possession of a DBP product or the book and or its corresponding "Medium" understand and agree not to use this said Copyright section to contradict this EULA, since this DBP product or book and its corresponding "Medium" are licensed and not sold.

NDPA 2B: Furthermore, you agree that as to this section, and subsection (d), of aforementioned U.S. Copyright Law, you are not permitted to post or sale or give-away or otherwise on the Internet or any other medium of communication or platform, or anywhere or place any DBP product and its "medium" without the exclusive notarized written authorization of the copyright owner and Publisher. That is, as to this EULA and its corresponding DBP product or book and its "Medium", The privileges prescribed by subsections (a) and (c) and (d) [of U.S. Copyright Section §109] do not apply to any DBP product and its "Mediums" since DBP products are licensed Not Sold and your privileges to access our DBP products and books and its "Medium" are limited as described in this EULA.

NDPA 3A: You understand and agree that the granted license, DBP products or this book, and its corresponding "Medium" CANNOT, at no time or place, by you or any other entity (besides the Publisher and a specified notarized authorized DBP Agent) be leased, licensed, sub-licensed, loaned, assign, conveyed, transferred, copied, reproduced, modified, adapted, merged, translated, given-away, rented, displayed and or announced to the public in any platform or way, or sold or otherwise distributed in any way, shape, form or format by you or any entity other than the Publisher and its specified notarized authorized DBP Agent, or as specified in this EULA.

You agree that Only the Publisher and the Publisher's designated Publisher Authorized Agents of any DBP product may provide distribution of "license" of DBP products or this book

and its corresponding "Medium" in accordance to this license agreement.

NDPA 3B: PROPRIETARY RIGHTS: Except where specifically stated otherwise in this EULA, you understand and agree that DBP owns all rights, titles and interest in and to all DBP products and their corresponding Medium including, without limitation, all intellectual and proprietary rights appurtenant thereto, and, except for the limited license granted to you herein, nothing in this EULA shall be construed to transfer, convey, impair or otherwise adversely affect DBP and its authors et al. ownership or proprietary rights therein or any other DBP information or materials, tangible or intangible, in any form and in any medium. All intellectual property rights, including copyright, patents, trademarks and trade secrets, are retained by the Publisher and its affiliates, licensors, and collaborators, all rights reserved.

You understand and agree that you may not copy, imitate or use the Trademarks et al., in whole or in part, for any purpose. No license or other right to use any Trademark et al. used or displayed on any of our mediums or marketing material is granted to You.

NDPA 3C: You understand and agree that **you may always view the Current List of Authorized Agents of DBP on its website or you can request a Current list at: MiCostaBella@Gmail.Com.** You further understand and agree that you will check the Current list of authorized Agents of DBP, before purchasing a DBP license, to make sure you are buying your license legally before you purchase any DBP license to access any DBP product and its corresponding medium.

NDPA 4-sub 1: You understand and agree and will honor that Darseli Book Publishing holds exclusive distribution rights of its products and corresponding mediums on any platform, the INTERNET or other electronic market places or similar electronic devises in addition to all non-Internet platforms.

You understand and agree that An editorial review or other similar opinion may reference the intellectual property in an article or news feed only so far as it does not imply any monetary gain for entity providing such news feed or book review article. Written request to do so can be made to the Publisher at: MiCostaBella@Gmail.Com. The exception would be a notarized written agreement with the Publisher in advance.

NDPA 4-sub 2: You understand and agree that All authorized license distribution Authorized Agent entities must agree with DBP on a Separate notarized written Agreement before the distribution entity is authorized to distribute any DBP license (including the DBP product's corresponding Publisher's medium {physical or non-physical cover and pages in paper format and/or electronic format, or otherwise containing a particular DBP product}) on behalf of the Publisher, and only after the granted distribution agent entity is on the "CURRENT AND UP-TO-DATE" DBP Authorized Agent List posted at Darseli.com website or by request of current agent list to MiCostaBella@Gmail.Com. This Agent List fluctuates (CHANGES) and so it is recommended to check the Updated Authorized DBP Agent List as indicated BEFORE DEALING WITH an apparent Publisher Authorized Agent or to make sure you are dealing with a Current and Valid Publisher Authorized Agent. Publisher Authorized License Reseller can be terminated by the Publisher at any time for any reason, especially in a violation of this EULA or its agreed commitments to DBP and general business integrity and ethical standards.

EULA SECTION LGR (Sec. 4 of 9): License Grant And Restrictions (LGR):

LGR 1-sub-1: YOU agree you will Not Transfer your license, lease or sublease your license, rent or license or sublicense your license, sale your license, assign your license, delegate or transfer or give-away your license rights of any DBP product, book (or e-book),or its Publisher owned "Medium" in any way or format or time or place (or in any format that may be conceived now or in the future). That is, you understand and agree that this limited DBP license is granted to you and you alone (license is exclusive to you only).

LGR 1-sub-2: YOU agree you will Not authorize another individual or entity to copy, reproduce, modify, adapt, merge, translate, assign, transfer or otherwise any DBP product or book and its corresponding "Medium" onto any computer or any other platform.

LGR 1-sub-3: You further agree and understand that the license granted to you pertains to only one corresponding DBP product and its corresponding "Medium" and no more. If you wish to purchase an additional license to have access to another single corresponding DBP product or book (and its "Medium"), you understand and agree that you must purchase another (separate) license to do so (allowing you access to that license's single corresponding book and DBP product and its corresponding "Medium").

LGR 2-sub-1: The book or DBP product is licensed to you generally for the "life" of the corresponding physical or electronic, or otherwise "Medium" or as to a specified time given by the Publisher at the time of ordering or acquiring from the Publisher or Publisher's authorized agent (so long as you abide by the EULA) as to this EULA or immediately terminate access if Publisher decides to revoke your license (and access to its corresponding DBP product and Medium) for any reason.

LGR 2-sub-2: You understand and agree that this license is revocable and can be Terminated by the Publisher at any time for any reason and without notice to you. Reason for termination may include your violation of this agreement or suspected violation of this agreement. At such time, you agree to surrender the book and its "Medium" (which is property of the Publisher at all times and places) to the Publisher or immediately destroy it if Publisher asks you to do so.

LGR 2-sub-3: You understand and agree that if you are No Longer interested in the DBP product or book during the period specified in the granted DBP product license, you acknowledge and agree that you will destroy the book and its corresponding "Medium" (or if e-Book or similar "Medium" format: delete the electronic file or similar file of the DBP product and its corresponding "Medium" provided).

LGR2-sub-4: You understand and agree that a DBP license purchaser can obtain their unique DBP license number by adding in sequence the unique DBP license serial number components using the following DBP license identifiers:

(1) The word or symbol "DBP" at beginning,
(2) followed by the YEAR, MONTH, DAY of DBP License purchase date,
(3) followed by one Family Name of DBP product license Purchaser,
(4) followed by the number of DBP licenses ordered in numerical digits (2 or more licenses listed as A1, B1, C1,... Ax, Bx, Cx,etc.)
(5) The DBP license Purchaser's Country of Origin as indicated,
(6) followed by the numerical date: 4-13-1950,
(7) and followed by and ended with the first (non-article) Word in the title of the corresponding DBP product.

You further agree that if the Publisher asks for this DBP license number, you will furnish it to the Publisher as an authentication of your DBP product license purchase. Accordingly, you agree to write this DBP product license number somewhere secure where you can access it if need be. **You also understand and agree that we may ask, and you will provide, additional identifiers to verify that you are the actual purchaser of the DBP product license.**

LGR 3: You agree that you are never allowed to obtain any tangible or intangible monetary or similar benefits for sharing unless otherwise specified in this EULA.

LGR 4: You further understand and agree that Only the Publisher or the Publisher's Authorized Agents (current authorized agents posted on the current DBP list at Darseli.Com or by request at MiCostaBella@Gmail.Com) are allowed to distribute a DBP product license, the DBP product and its corresponding license-only Publisher "Medium" which belongs to Publisher at all times and places.

LGR 5: Non-Profit public libraries (herein herewith also known as "public library" or "public libraries" or "library" or "libraries") are the ONLY ENTITY permitted in this license agreement to allow their patrons to check out "share" the book and its "medium", FREE OF CHARGE, as a form of sharing the book so long as the book is returned to the original licensed entity (the public library that purchased a corresponding license to a single corresponding book from the Publisher).

LGR 5 sub-1: Aforementioned Libraries CANNOT sell, lease, sublease, license, sub-license, give away, rent, rent for monetary gain, copy, reproduce, modify, adapt, or otherwise the License, the book or DBP product, and its corresponding "Medium" at ANYTIME for any reason including if the public library decides to discard the book and its "Medium": in such cases the book (or DBP product) and its corresponding "Medium" must be destroyed by the library holding a corresponding DBP license, or return, at its expense, to the Publisher the DBP product and its corresponding Medium. If the said medium is in electronic or similar format, the library agrees to delete or otherwise destroy the DBP product's licensed medium.

LGR 7 sub-2A: All other restrictions in this DBP product license agreement apply directly to public libraries as well. If the public library does not agree fully with this EULA or any part of this agreement, they are not permitted to purchase a license of a DBP product or book or to acquire (by any means) a DBP product or the book and its corresponding "Medium".

LGR 8: EDUCATOR PRIVILEGES as to a DBP license: A credentialed, certificated educator may share the book or DBP product and its corresponding medium with his or her assigned students during school hours within the school on-site physical classroom. Students must be supervised at all time by the DBP license purchaser (educator) when using any DBP product including books and their corresponding medium. Students may not borrow the book as it is to remain with the educator (who purchased the DBP product license) at all times. And said DBP license purchaser is responsible for the acts of the students that go against the interest of the Publisher and its intellectual property and corresponding mediums and the EULA. The "Educator" DBP license purchaser understands and agrees that Any violation by students against this EULA makes the "EDUCATOR" purchaser of a DBP license fully liable.
LGR 9: The DBP product License does not allow the DBP product to be used on more than one "Medium" other than that provided to you by the Publisher or its authorized agent at time of license purchase, and you understand and agree that you may not make the book or DBP product available over additional physical "Medium" formats or electronic "Medium" formats or any other type of "Medium" formats or any type of network where it could be used by multiple people or devices or multiple computers at the same time or stand-alone. This DBP product License does not grant you any rights to share the DBP issued license, the book or DBP product and its corresponding "Medium" other than those explicitly stated in this Agreement.

EULA SECTION T (Sec. 5 of 9): Termination (T1)

T1: The Publisher, Darseli Book Publishing, may, at its sole discretion and without notice, terminate your DBP product license for ANY REASON effective immediately. Such license termination by the Publisher terminates your access to use the single corresponding DBP product and its corresponding "Medium" (Medium owned by the Publisher at all times and places). Upon Termination stated, you understand and agree that you are not entitled to any compensation or refund of any kind due to said termination or otherwise. You also agree that Upon termination of your license by Publisher you must immediately stop using the book or DBP product and its "Medium" and destroy the DBP product and its corresponding "Medium", or return them to the Publisher (at your own shipping expense). If the book or DBP product and its "Medium" is in digital format or similar format, then you are instructed to immediately delete the DBP product and its corresponding "medium" from your hard drive or other storage mechanism or constructs or otherwise upon termination of your license.
T2: If in turn you wish to terminate (end) an issued license and this license agreement of a DBP product or book (such termination by you effectively and immediately terminates your access to the book or DBP product and its corresponding "Medium"), you must immediately destroy or return (at your own shipping expense) to Publisher the book and its "Medium" as described above. The balance of the Agreement shall survive any such 'termination of license rights'. You are not entitled to a license fee refund upon termination unless specified differently in this license agreement.

EULA SECTION LPMA (Sec. 6 of 9): License Fee Payment And Modification Agreement (LPMA):

LPMA 1: You agree and understand that the DBP product license to be issued to you (and possession of its single corresponding book and its Publisher's "medium"), upon and after your agreement of this EULA license agreement, requires payment to the Publisher or its authorized agent at the current set "License Fee" amount, or license fee amount presented to you, for the completion of a DBP product license issuance to you.
LPMA 2: Certain book or DBP product license issuances by Publisher to particular individuals or organizations are granted without a license fee for the sole purpose of promotional review of the book and its "Medium". Such granted DBP product licenses to these particular individuals or organizations by the Publisher are also bound to this license agreement and its sections in its entirety (which includes non-transferable rules of the license, the book or its Publisher owned "Medium" or selling of book or DBP product or otherwise transferring DBP products in violation of this DBP product license agreement). If aforementioned particular entity receiving from the Publisher such a DBP product license with its corresponding book and its "medium" in this way does not fully agree with this EULA license agreement, then their granted license is immediately revoked and they agree that they must immediately return (at their shipping expense) or destroy their provided licensed DBP product and its corresponding "Medium", and all other parts of this license agreement survive.
LPMA 3: You understand and agree that The Publisher reserves the right to modify this agreement (EULA) at any time to reflect, for example but not limited to, and without notice, changes in our business or to maintain a DBP product or book in a license ONLY format. If DBP modifies this EULA agreement a revised version will be posted on our website www.darseli.com and/or our official social web pages or you may request the current EULA by email to: MiCostaBella@Gmail.Com. You agree that your continued use of any of our DBP products and books and their corresponding "Medium" will constitute your acceptance of the modified agreement that can be made at any time and without notice other than posting a revised agreement on one of our official web pages or our other public notice platforms at our option or by you requesting a revised EULA via email as stated.
If you do not agree with the DBP revised license agreement (EULA) changes allowing you to have continued access to any of our DBP products or books and their respective corresponding "Medium" in your possession or to be in your possession, you herewith agree to destroy or return the DBP product and its corresponding "Medium" (shipping expense belongs to you) to the Publisher (or its authorized agent) without a refund or any other sort of compensation to you.

EULA SECTION LLLA (Sec. 7 of 9): Language and Law Of License Agreement (LLLA):

LLLA 1: The controlling language of this agreement is in English ONLY. Any translation of this license agreement to any other language besides English that you may have received is provided only for your convenience. You understand and agree If any discrepancies are found in language translation of this EULA, the controlling language of this EULA is English always.
LLLA 2A: Controlling Law and Severability: This license is to be governed by the State of Washington, U.S.A. If any part of this agreement is found void and unenforceable by a legitimate government entity court, it will not affect the validity of the balance of this agreement, which will remain valid and enforceable according to its terms. This agreement may only be modified in writing by the Publisher: Darseli Book Publishing (DBP). Again, the English version of this agreement will be the ONLY version used when interpreting or construing this agreement.
LLLA 2B: You irrevocably and unconditionally (a) consent to submit to the exclusive jurisdiction of the state and federal courts of King County, Washington for any litigation or disputed arising out of or related to this Agreement, (b) you agree not to commence any litigation arising out of or related to this Agreement except in the state or federal courts mentioned herein, (c) you agree not to plead or claim that such litigation brought therein has been brought in an inconvenient forum. (d) EACH PARTY (you and the Publisher and any other unforeseen entity) HEREBY WAIVES ITS RIGHT TO A JURY TRIAL IN CONNECTION WITH ANY DISPUTE OR LEGAL PROCEEDING ARISING OUT OF THIS AGREEMENT OR THE SUBJECT MATTER HEREOF and THEREOF.
LLLA 3: COMPLIANCE WITH EXPORT LAWS. You may not use or otherwise export or re-export any DBP product except as authorized by the Publisher and the United States law and the laws of the jurisdiction in which the DBP product was obtained. In particular, but without limitation, any DBP product may not be exported or re-exported (a) into any U.S. embargoed countries or (b) to anyone on the U.S. Treasury Department's list of Specially Designated Nationals or the U.S. Department of Commerce Denied Person's List or Entity List. By using any DBP product as licensed to you and specified in this EULA, you represent and warrant that you are not located in any such country or on any such list. You also agree that you will not use any DBP product for any purposes prohibited by United States of America law.
LLLA 4: The DBP product License Provided by Authorized Third Parties:
The Publisher does not control, endorse, or accept responsibility for Any third party services. Any dealings between you and any authorized or unauthorized third party in connection with a Third Party Service or sell, including such party's privacy policies and use of your personal information, delivery of and payment for licenses fees and services, and any other terms, conditions, warranties, or representations associated with such dealings, are solely between you and such third party. Any DBP authorized third party agent must always abide by DBP's EULA and additional notarized agreements between authorized 3rd Party Agent and DBP. Any third party Authorized distributor of a DBP product license, as an agent for the Publisher, agrees to abide by its separate agreement with Publisher and also to abide by the Publisher's EULA outlined here. No third party is permitted to violate any Publisher sections in this agreement. Furthermore, any agent of the Publisher is to abide by all laws in the region in which it resides in so far as it does not violate this license agreement and the additional separate license agreement with Publisher. If you purchased a license of a DBP product via an authorized 3rd Party DBP agent and cannot find a suitable resolution to your issue, please bring it up directly to the Publisher at MiCostaBella@Gmail.Com. The Publisher will do its best to attempt to resolve your issue.
LLLA 5: Equitable Relief. You hereby fully agree that any breach of this Agreement by you, including any unauthorized disclosure of Confidential Information or specific sections in this Agreement, would cause irreparable harm to the Publisher, and that in the event of any breach or threatened breach of this agreement, The Publisher will be entitled to obtain equitable relief in addition to any other remedy. Publisher's rights and remedies under this Agreement shall be cumulative and not exclusive of any other rights or remedies provided hereunder or by law.

EULA SECTION OA (Sec. 8 of 9):: Other Agreements (OA)

OA 1: Indemnity. You, and or possessor of DBP products and their corresponding "Mediums", agree to defend and indemnify and hold harmless the Publisher (DBP) and its authors and employees or contracted employees, officers, directors, agents, successors, assigns, and affiliates from any and all liabilities, losses, actions, damages, settlements, or claims (including all reasonable expenses, costs, and attorneys' fees) out of or relating to your use of, or any reliance on, any DBP products including this DBP product and its corresponding "Medium" or service of a DBP product. Your use of any DBP products including this DBP product and its corresponding "Medium" are used AT YOUR OWN RISK.
OA 3: Intellectual Property Rights; No Modifications. You acknowledge and agree that this and any DBP product and its corresponding "Medium", and the trademarks associated with the DBP product, and its corresponding "Medium" are the intellectual property owned by the Publisher (DBP), and/or the author of the DBP product or book or its illustrators. DBP, the authors, et al. reserve all of their respective rights under such applicable laws. All DBP products are protected by Copyright, Trademark, et al., including without limitation, by United States Copyright Law, international treaty provisions, and applicable laws in the jurisdiction of use.

EULA SECTION G (Sec. 9 of 9): General (G):

G 1: This license Agreement of the specified DBP product or any DBP product, herewith, herein, including Additional Terms below, is the Entire Agreement between you (the licensee or to be licensee {or entity in possession of a DBP product} granted access to the DBP product by way of DBP license with license fee payment made or otherwise acquired) and the Publisher (DBP): and replaces all prior understandings, communications and agreements, oral or written (with the exception of additional notarized Agent-Publisher separate agreement or other notarized agreement with the Publisher). If any court of law, having the jurisdiction, rules that any part of this Agreement is not consistent with its laws: that part of the that agreement will be formally removed without affecting the remainder of the License Agreement (EULA) which shall continue in full force and effect.
G 2: Additionally, You understand and agree that if the Publisher does not agree with a court of law decision, the Publisher may revoke your license and henceforth end your privilege to any DBP product (intellectual property) and its corresponding "Medium". In such an event, the licensee entity of a DBP product or holder of the corresponding "medium" of the DBP product, you, shall immediately return (at licensee's and or holder's own shipping expense) or destroy the DBP product and its corresponding "medium" in its, her, his possession immediately.
G 2-sub 1: You understand and agree that The United Nations Convention on Contracts for the International Sale of Goods does Not apply to this Agreement (the application of which is expressly excluded). You cannot loan, assign, delegate, sell, rent, convey, transfer, copy, reproduce, modify, adapt, merge, translate or otherwise dispose of, whether voluntarily or involuntarily, by operation of law or otherwise, or transfer ownership of this Agreement and license (AND its book and corresponding Publisher's owned "Medium") to anyone without written approval from the Publisher or as instructed in this EULA. However, the Publisher may assign or transfer license (and its corresponding book and "Medium") without your consent or notice to an authorized affiliate, similar, or whom ever the Publisher wishes to designate at any time and place.
G 3: UNIQUE LICENSE NUMBER. Each DBP product and its corresponding "Medium" has a unique license number (as described earlier in this EULA). The license number is set to correspond directly to a purchaser of the license in order to access the single corresponding book and its Publisher owned "Medium". This Unique License number is also kept at the Publisher's Databases corresponding to an exact purchaser of a DBP product license. That is, the License is a unique 1 to 1 correspondence: Publisher granting license and corresponding license number to One Licensee corresponding to a single DBP product and its corresponding Publisher owned "Medium". This license number is non-transferable at any time or place unless otherwise stated in this agreement. And, you understand and agree that you are to keep this license number Confidential for security reasons between the Publisher and You.
G 3 sub-1: If the "medium" of any DBP product comes into a possession of someone or an entity other than the original purchaser of the license, it is here advised that such entity in possession of any DBP product and its corresponding "medium" is not allowed to access the DBP product (intellectual property) or its corresponding Publisher owned "medium". Henceforth, such an entity without authorization to access a DBP product is herewith advised to immediately destroy the DBP product and its corresponding "medium" to avoid legal remedies on behalf of the Publisher for violation of the book's EULA, licensing only distribution format, and other legal rights.

G4: This EULA license agreement wording ends on this written line.

這本書致力於...

瑪麗亞路易莎 阿維萊斯 菲耶羅 Larrinaga 麥德林

瑪麗亞路易斯是一個充滿愛心的人,她關心並幫助她遇到的任何人。
她也是一位敬業的母親和婆婆。

瑪麗亞・路易莎 瑪麗亞路易莎 孜孜不倦地工作以支持她的 六 個孩子:
(伊麗莎白、南內特、塞西莉亞、戴安娜、阿方索和貝爾納多)。

她是一個很棒的人,她也幫助了她的同胞。
她特別幫助了加利福尼亞州聖莫尼卡的無家可歸者。

瑪麗亞路易莎 是一位視覺藝術家,他幫助完成了第一個視覺概念化
這本兒童讀物:飢餓的蜘蛛朱利安。

謝謝阿比!

和阿比一樣,本書的作者也想方設法幫助人類。

最近,作者遇到了一個人道主義組織。該組織旨在通過與其他人一起尋找
可行的解決方案並向社區提出這些解決方案來減輕人類痛苦的問題。
這個組織的好處是 它不接受任何 財政捐助。與本組織的努力相關的所有費
用均由成員根據其 能力和意願自行單獨直接支 付。

要查看這位作者的發現並考慮加入,請訪問:

Eternoi.Com

Eternoi 人道主義組織 (Eternoi)

從前,住著一隻白蜘蛛,它一直在挨餓。
名叫朱利安的白蜘蛛住在兒童房的一個小盒子裡

幾天來, 這只獨行蜘蛛渴望食物。

一天,白蜘蛛因為飢餓,決定從盒子裡出來,開始尋找食物。

當白蜘蛛用它的八條長腿爬上盒子，穿過頂部的一個小洞時，他看到了食物。
這是一個草莓果凍三明治，放在一張小木桌上，旁邊是一張小床。

白蜘蛛爬上了小木桌。當他把目光投向果凍三明治時：他渴望它的每一部分。

孤零零的白蜘蛛從來沒有吃過果凍三明治,也不敢吃,怕會生病。然而他太餓了,對他來說已經無所謂了:他吃了第一口。第一口咬完後,他迅速咀嚼剩下的果凍三明治,直到什麼都沒有了。
NOTHING left!!!:) NADA LEFT!!!!:) NADA RIGHT!!!:)

白獨蛛朱利安吃了這麼多食物,變得又胖又圓。當他慢慢地爬下桌子時,朱利安的蜘蛛繩開始斷裂,因為朱利安(孤獨的白蜘蛛)吃了整個三明治後的重量。

當他完全從空中降落到地面時：孤零零的白蜘蛛朱利安緩緩地穿過房間，爬回了他在盒子裡的家。

可是當他到達盒子時,他無法穿過他用作門的洞!他又胖又圓,洞不再大到讓他穿不進去。

朱利安坐在箱子上思考這個問題。過了一會兒，他想出了一個主意。他的想法是屏住呼吸足夠長的時間，讓他能夠穿過這個洞（大約一個美國鎳的大小）。

經過長時間的掙扎，朱利安終於把自己擠進了洞裡。[優秀的朱利安！很高興您找到了解決方案！:)]

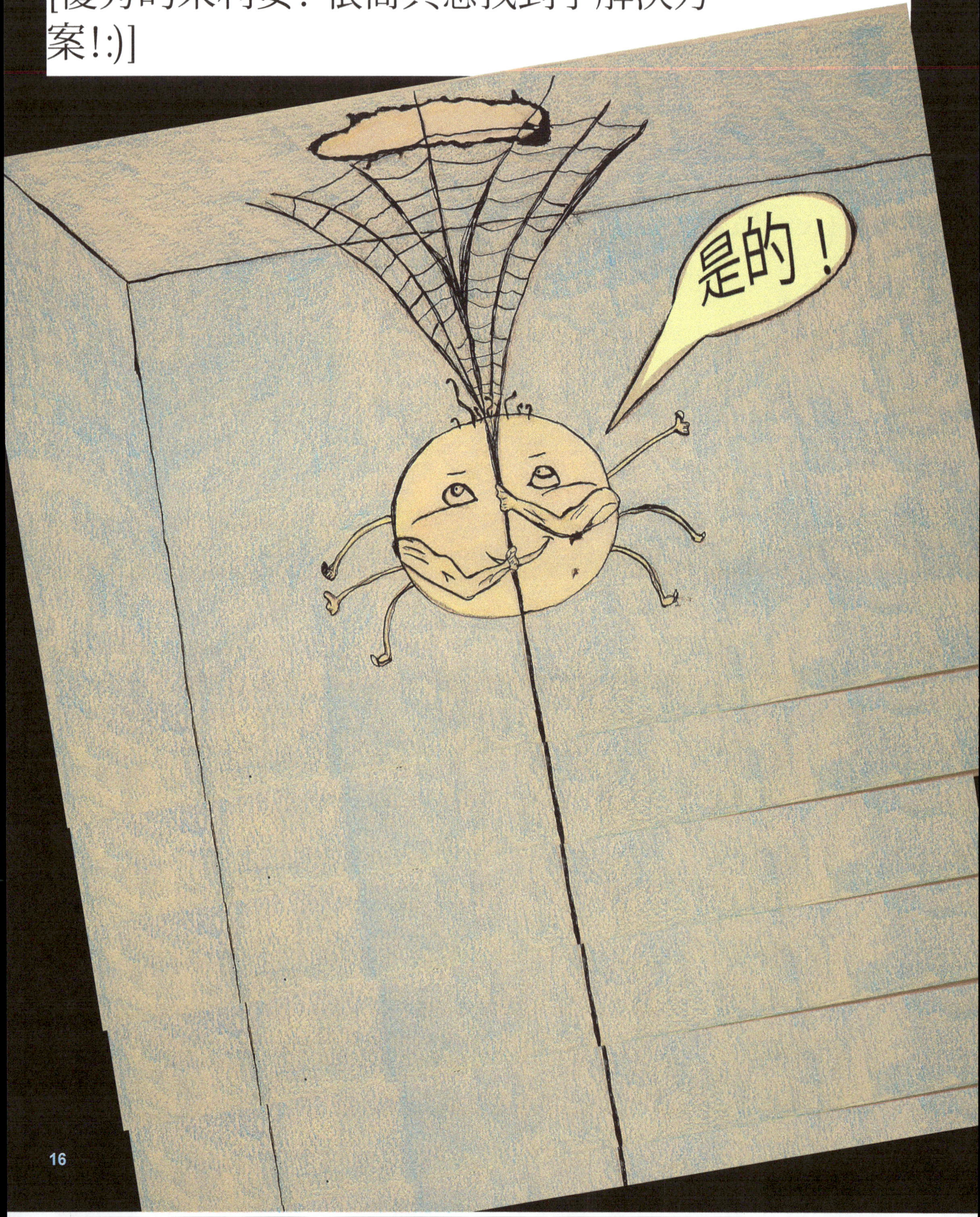

就在朱利安悄悄地從視線中消失時，馬科斯（住在房間裡的男孩）走進了房間。當男孩伸手去抓他的果凍三明治時，他什麼也沒抓住！GRABBED NOTHING!!!! ¡NADA!

"我的三明治呢?"他大叫!馬科斯對他的三明治消失感到驚訝和憤怒。"誰拿走了我的三明治?"他問自己。他終於得出結論,
他的母親是不小心把它拿走了。他決定不再想他的單一果凍三明治,然後上床睡覺。

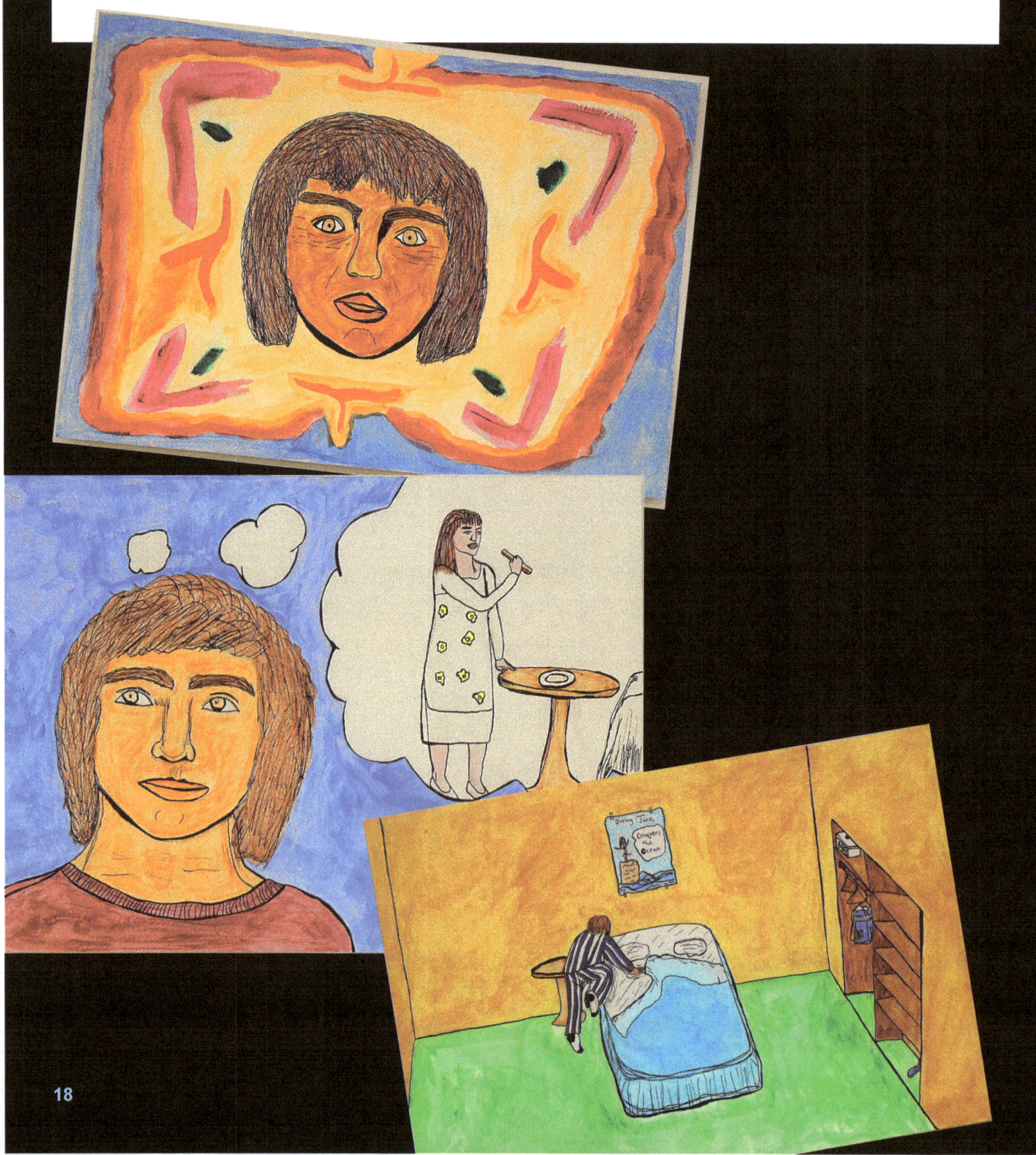

就在朱利安悄悄地從視線中消失時，馬科斯（住在房間裡的男孩）走進了房間。當男孩伸手去抓他的果凍三明治時，他什麼也沒抓住！GRABBED NOTHING!!!! ¡NADA!

"我的三明治呢?"他大叫!馬科斯對他的三明治消失感到驚訝和憤怒。"誰拿走了我的三明治?"他問自己。他終於得出結論,
他的母親是不小心把它拿走了。他決定不再想他的單一果凍三明治,然後上床睡覺。

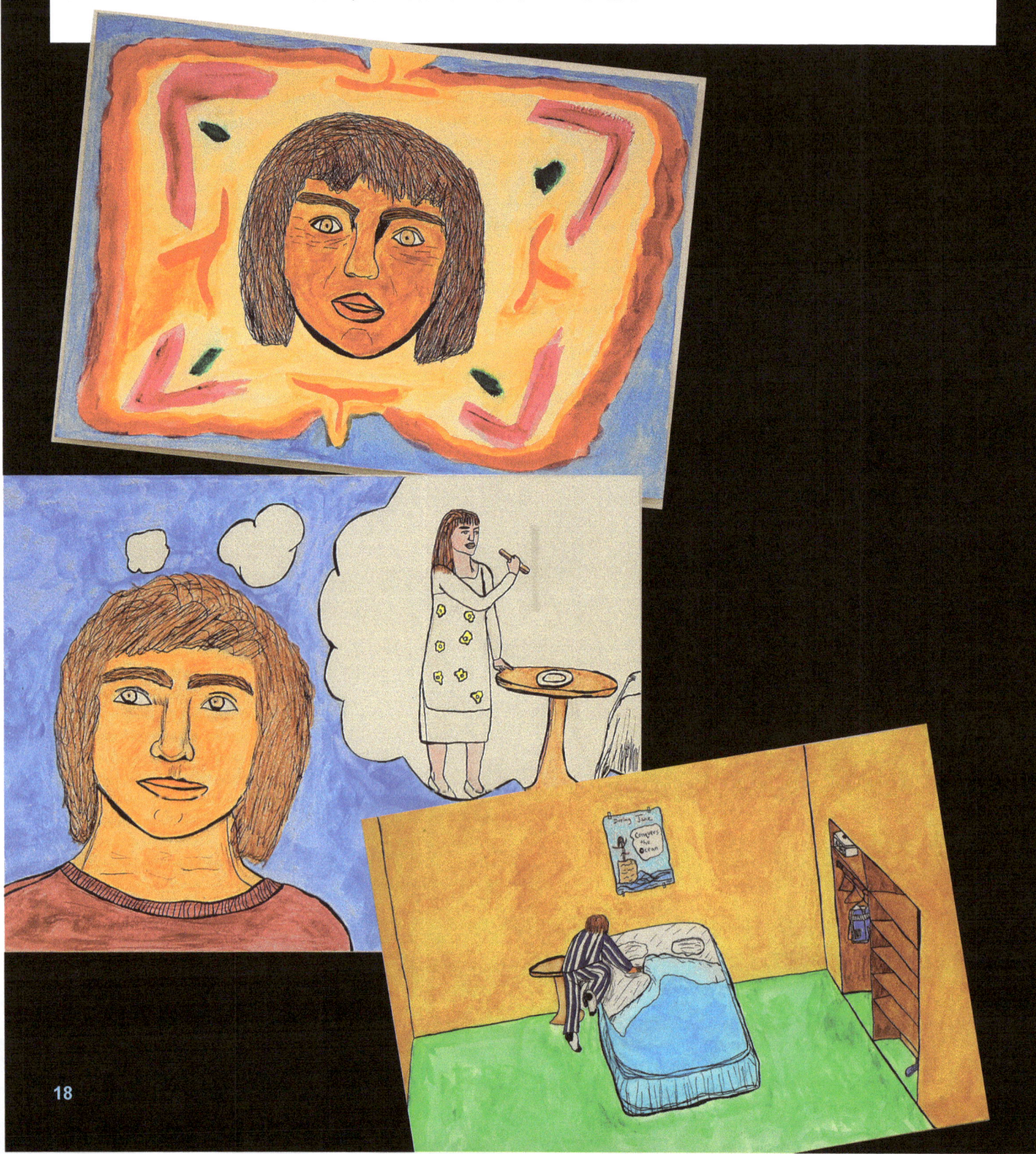

第二天,當他在浴室時,同樣的事情發生了。
這次他很不高興,因為他真的很想在睡覺前吃掉他的果凍三明治。馬科斯決定下樓去和他媽媽談談他的果凍三明治失踪的事情。

當馬科斯來到廚房時,他的母親正在清洗碗碟。"媽媽!你是不是從我房間裡拿了我的果凍三明治?!"他相當嚴厲地問她。"不,馬科斯,我沒有拿走你的果凍三明治。為什麼?" "我的三明治連續第二個晚上沒了!我上廁所的時候把果凍三明治留在了小木桌上。當我回到我的房間時,我的果凍三明治不見了!!!" GONE!!!!":(

"也許你在去洗手間之前吃了你的果凍三明治。"他媽媽若有所思地說。馬科斯抗議:"媽媽！它怎麼會連續發生兩次而我卻沒有意識到呢？
馬科斯開始懷疑自己,他說(試圖讓自己平靜下來):"嗯……也許它就像你說的那樣發生了。"明天我會努力提高警惕。"說完,馬科斯就上床睡覺了。

第三天,馬科斯去洗手間的時候,提醒自己三明治還在桌子上。

當他回到他的房間時,他的三明治不見了!馬科斯勃然大怒,吼道:"誰吃了我的三明治?!!!"沒有人回答。在馬科斯從浴室回來之前,朱利安(白蜘蛛)已經在包廂裡回到了他的家。朱利安不懂馬科斯的人際交流。男孩發出的聲音,對他來說,只是盒子外面傳來的震動。

outside of the box!!!

馬科斯隨即下定決心,為小偷設下圈套!"明天我們就看誰會後悔。"馬科斯一邊想著自己的計劃,一淘氣地狠的說道。

與此同時，朱利安感覺不舒服。他的肚子疼得厲害。"啊啊啊啊啊啊啊啊啊啊啊啊啊啊啊啊啊啊啊啊啊啊啊啊啊啊啊啊啊啊啊啊啊啊啊啊啊！"他抱怨道。"可能是我吃多了？"他心想。"但因為我通常吃一個完整的果凍三明治，所以不能吃太多。"，他用蜘蛛語補充道！

想了一會兒他的問題：他想到了一個主意。"我知道它是什麼！是果凍三明治裡的花生醬。嗚嗚——嗚嗚——不！"他不滿地嘟嚷著。"如果裡面有花生醬，我再也不會吃果凍三明治了！呸呸呸呸！" **Yucky yuck yuck!!!**"

早上,經過夜間多次嘔吐和上廁所後,他感覺好多了。[對你有好處,朱利安!:)]

第四天晚些時候,朱利安從包廂裡爬出來,走向馬科斯床邊小木桌上的果凍三明治。

當他走近三明治時，朱利安能聞到裡面有花生醬的味道。"不不不不！我不吃這個！"，朱利安說。於是他一口沒吃就回到了包廂。

當馬科斯從浴室回到他的房間時，他注意到桌子上的所有東西都是一樣的。他布下的陷阱還沒有被觸發

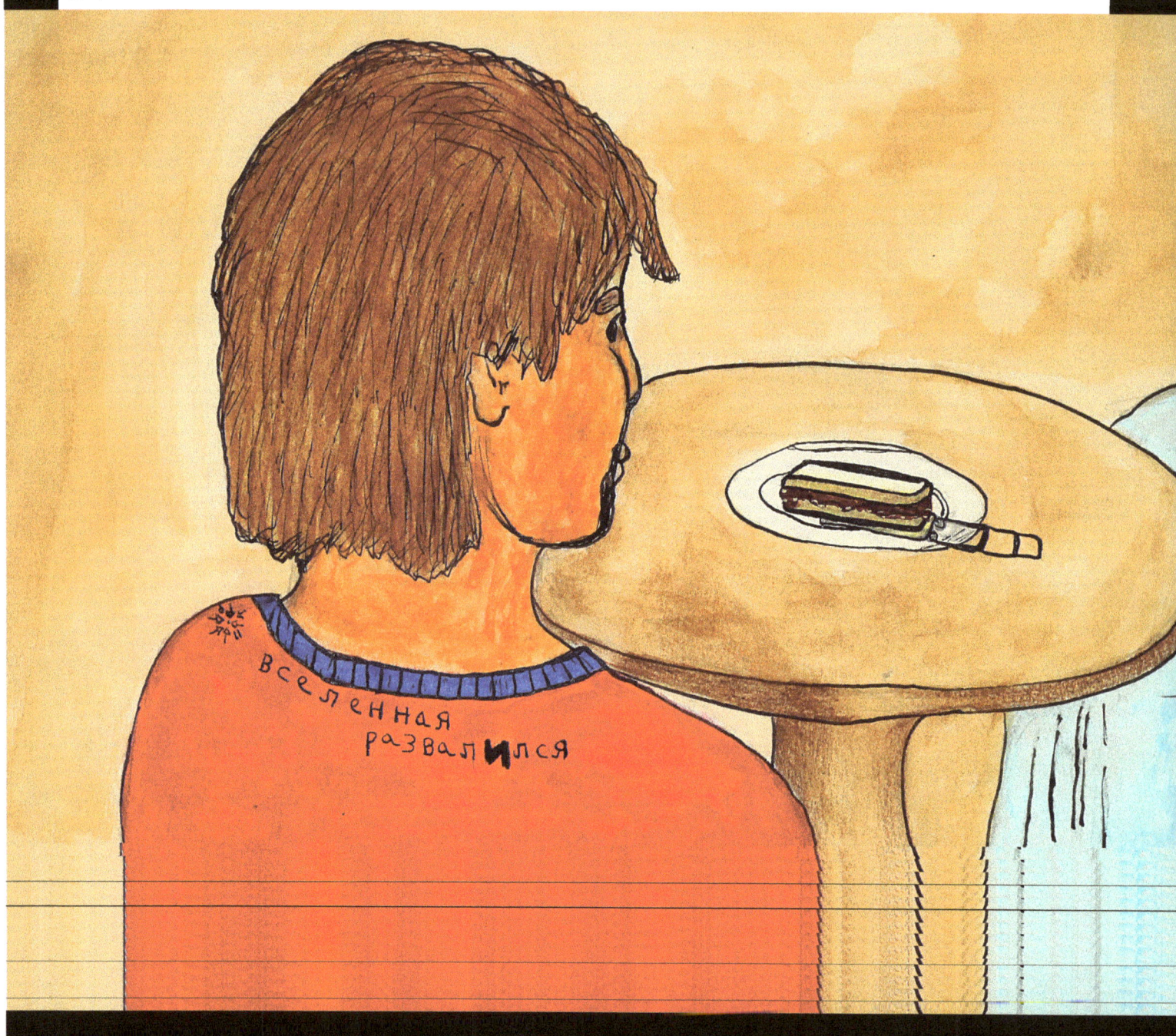

然後他決定躲在門和梳妝台之間等待小偷。

馬科斯等了好一會兒,又繼續等了好一會兒。而且,他還等了很久!他等了那麼久,終於睡著了。 *fell asleep.*

幾個小時後，他醒了。馬科斯有點餓，看到小木桌上的三明治，就伸手去拿。he reached for it.

當他拿起它時，陷阱被觸發，陷阱的鋼棒在他的手指上折斷。"哦哦哦！！！"馬科斯大聲尖叫！他忘記了放在三明治下面的陷阱。the **trap** that he had placed underneath the sandwich.

當馬科斯的母親聽到尖叫聲時，她跑上樓梯看看發生了什麼事。當她進入時，她看到馬科斯痛苦地被陷阱牢牢地套在右手的手指上。"這裡到底發生了什麼？你是怎麼對自己這樣的？"當他的母親從他的手指上取下陷阱時，馬科斯感覺好多了。"對不起媽媽，我錯了。我設置了一個陷阱來抓捕一直在吃我的果凍三明治的小偷。但他從來沒有來過。在我等待的時候，我睡著了。當我醒來時，我餓了。所以，我伸手去拿我的三明治：我不記得我放在果凍三明治下面的陷阱了。

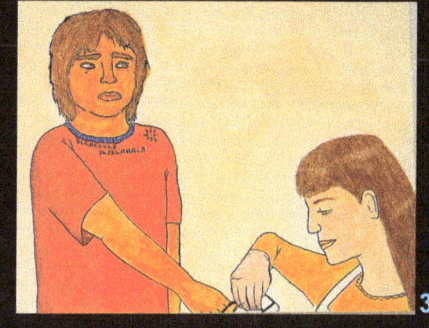

第二天,馬科斯在廚房的桌子上吃了他的三明治。他和他的母親一起決定,他最好在上樓回房間之前在廚房裡吃完他的果凍三明治。

日子一天天過去，白蜘蛛越來越餓。他沒有東西吃，因為房間裡已經沒有食物了。他必須做點什麼！:(Julian had to do SOMETHING!!!!

他想著要解決的問題。終於，他想到了一個主意。"我需要搬出房間去別處尋找食物"。
Julian had to move-out of the room and search-for-food elsewhere.:

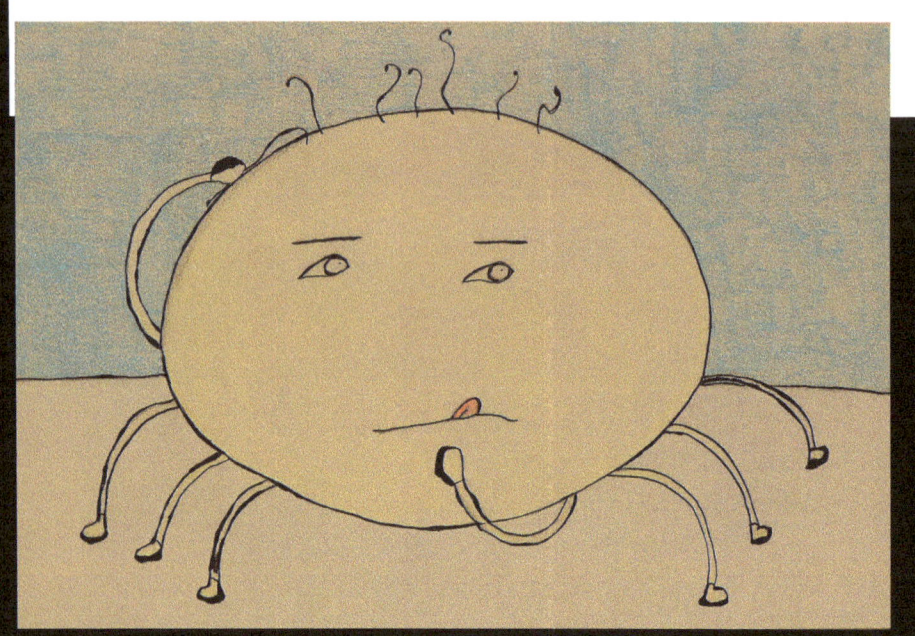

朱利安認為這個想法是最好的做法，所以他就這麼做了。他從包廂裡爬出來，走向窗戶，開始了他的旅程。希望運氣好，他想找到一個有他最喜歡的食物的地方：白麵包草莓果凍三明治!:) [哦，好吃!:)]

終

"感謝讀者花時間閱讀我的生活如何開始的故事！祝你永遠平安快樂！"

最良好的祝愿，

朱利安